For the Remington Family

THE
ESSENCE
OF
MOMENTS

Poems by

Robert H. Deluty

GATEWAY PRESS, INC.
Baltimore, MD   2004

Please direct all correspondence and book orders to:
Robert H. Deluty
4783 Ilkley Moor Lane
Ellicott City, Maryland 21043

Library of Congress Control Number 2004110669
ISBN 0-9704201-8-8

Published by
Gateway Press, Inc.
1001 N. Calvert Street
Baltimore, MD 21202-3897

Printed in the United States of America

To
Robert Spiess, Art Bounds,
Tim Scannell, David Priebe,
and Winnie Cross

Other books by Robert H. Deluty
published by Gateway Press

Within and Between: Poems (2000)
The Long and Short of It: Essays and Poems (2003)
Observed and Imagined: Poems and Essays (2004)

Contents

8   still-grieving child
     grade school recital
     Maryland hopscotch
     on the rear bumpers
     student athlete

9   renowned orator
     MIT grad
     ten-year-old linguist
     calculus exam
     conservationist

10   Out of their League
     Hope

11   evening course
     driving eighty-five
     summer road paver
     demented father
     Yom Kippur

12   a broken shoelace
     misbehaving child
     college sophomore
     at *Tiffany's*
     airplane-phobic man

13   unprepared student
     Chinese immigrant
     Baylor lecture hall
     city sidewalk
     ninth inning, tied game

14   her six-year-old son
     drug counselor
     old world polyglot
     his son's fiancée
     great-great grandfather

60　flight to Utah
college weightlifter
center fielder
inept mugger
full-bearded man

61　after the death
poor family
their sixteen-year-old
biology class
his father bragging

62　during the exam
Russian immigrant
her twelve-year-old
over dinner
sorting through

63　ornithologist
delivery boy
first-year resident
desperately
two worriers wed

64　before the midterm
run-down diner
early morning class
on his lunch break
kosher deli

65　again late for school
psychotic man
first encounter
adored grandfather
after breakfast

The Essence of Moments

Haiku: A poem recording the essence of a moment keenly perceived, in which nature is linked to human nature. Usually a haiku in English is written in three unrhymed lines of seventeen or fewer syllables.

Haiku Society of America (1994)

While it is similar to haiku in form, senryu is different in effect ... it relies on wit, irony, and satire to comment on the human condition.

Lee Gurga (2003)

Haiku and Senryu are miniature poems which give expression to sudden or subtle moments of curious awareness and insight into the nature of passing time ... There is a pause, either punctuated or implied, after either the first or second phrase (sometimes in the midst of the second line) ... which serves as the axis of the experience, the moment coming into focus. The expression is achieved with phrases that suggest more than they state, allowing the reader's imagination to rhapsodize and make the connections and fill in the colors.

David Priebe (2004)

eighthieth birthday ...
identical twin brothers
wearing the same smile

little leaguer
stationed in right field
picking wildflowers

placing crank calls
to a hair-weaving salon ...
three chemo patients

elderly smokers
chatting about the doctors
they have outlived

two Nobel winners
deciding who pays for lunch ～
rock, paper, scissors

Las Vegas chapel …
a faux-Elvis preacher weds
a drunken couple

HOV lane …
a solitary driver
and a Christmas crèche

old tobacco pouch
filled with the memories
of her late father

son of musicians
mortifying his parents
pursues law school

cemetery …
beside his grandson's grave
sadness defeats rage

his father, post stroke …
a soaring eagle tattoo
on a withered arm

fourth of July …
under the night's fireworks
lightning bugs dancing

windshield wipers
working on a sunny day …
cicada summer

Haitian immigrant
trying to comprehend
bulimia

dirt-phobic woman
becoming desensitized
in her son's bedroom

haiku poet
choosing his Lotto numbers:
five, seven, five

army colonel …
his obit photo presents
a teenaged cadet

college dorm room …
beneath a short table leg
last year's physics text

farmer's granddaughter
in Gucci bib overalls
reclaiming her roots

put on hold
by his tax auditor ~
blues music playing

recycle day ...
hopes to impress his neighbors
with French wine bottles

mother of seven
mending threadbare pajamas
for the new baby

still dreaming
of a major league career ...
ninety-year-old fan

fiftieth birthday ...
wishing her children good health,
herself no drooping

teen compromising:
two belly button piercings
for no tattoos

still-grieving child
says goodbye to her Dad's suits
a decade later

grade school recital ...
obese dancers elicit
loudest ovation

Maryland hopscotch ...
avoiding the cicadas
on city sidewalks

on the rear bumpers
of their Japanese cars
Old Glory stickers

student athlete
taking the elevator ...
two-story building

renowned orator
yet again rendered speechless
by his teenaged son

MIT grad
placing his tassled cap
on his grandmother

ten-year-old linguist
learning how to say *buttocks*
in twelve languages

calculus exam ...
professor pens a red F
and a frowny face

conservationist
collecting Laundromat lint
for future pillows

Out of their League

Observing
the Nobel laureate in physics
posing questions
to an overwhelmed sophomore

His colleague
is reminded of Sandy Koufax
hurling fastballs
to a Met hitting .204

Hope

Morbidly obese,
Dateless for decades,
Spends her spare time
Recording televised
Concerts and miniseries.
Asked why, she responds
They will be gifts
For my children.

evening course ...
professor eating dinner
during the midterm

driving eighty-five
with the windows rolled down
drying his hair

summer road paver
listening to his daughter
complain that she's bored

demented father
unable to comprehend
his children's tears

Yom Kippur ...
guilt-ridden Jew at *Denny's*
orders dry toast

a broken shoelace …
his daughter inserting
mint dental floss

misbehaving child
hiding in a clothes closet
bargains with God

college sophomore
taking on *Finnegans Wake*
with a hangover

at *Tiffany's*
pro middle linebacker
choosing one earring

airplane-phobic man
relieved to be seated
beside two nuns

unprepared student
hoping his beloved teacher
has a minor stroke

Chinese immigrant
staring at his teen grandson ...
a spiked blond mohawk

Baylor lecture hall ...
Jewish prof defines *chutzpah*
for his Baptist class

city sidewalk ...
in front of a boarded house
an old woman sweeps

ninth inning, tied game ...
baby and her grandfather
sleeping soundly

her six-year-old son
saving dirt from his sneakers
for a rainy day

drug counselor
and her teenaged client
compare pierced tongues

old world polyglot
reserving his best Yiddish
for the right insult

his son's fiancée ...
tattooed on her ankle
Heaven's above

great-great-grandfather
placing a ten-inch taper
on his birthday cake

rabid Cubs fan
demanding that her first-born
be named Sosa

hijacked airplane ...
a passenger takes out
his daughter's photo

centenarian
accounting for her long life:
I never married

finding in the sleeve
of his now-pink shirt
one magenta sock

Orthodox Jew
eyeing a cheeseburger ...
lust trumping guilt

philanderer's grave
surrounded by the tombstones
of mistresses/wives

immigrant mother
forbidding her children
to use spell-check

ten-year-old boy
trying to stretch out
his one chest hair

eye doctor smiles
noting his patient's job:
baseball umpire

screaming two-year-old
knocks over a water glass
holding Grandma's teeth

at the reunion
mistaking her great-grandson
for her first-born

Passover ends ...
Jewish teen speed-dialing
Papa John's Pizza

on the beach at dusk
searching through sand, shells ∼
a lost contact lens

two lovebirds
tugging opposite ends
of a wayward worm

eliciting
appreciative gasps ...
thonged sunbather

Haiku is not in the business of trying to discover totally new things (that is the province of science) but in perceiving things in a totally new way (which is poetry).

Robert Spiess (1999)

Make everything as simple as possible, but not simpler.

Albert Einstein (attributed; source unknown)

ten-year-old card shark
winning the largest pot
with a pair of fours

psychoanalyst
biting his lower lip
to stay awake

one year married ~
unable to remember
their first dance

Jewish mother frets …
her actor son earns more
than her doctor son

midterm taker
staring at the ceiling more
than at his exam

after the briss
baby's four-year-old brother
requests the foreskin

formal wedding ...
the best man sporting a tux
and black flip-flops

doctor's waiting room ...
elderly men discussing
the price of caskets

Jewish man worries
whether a fast is broken
by using mouthwash

haiku instructor
betting on the fifth horse
in the seventh race

district spelling bee ...
a contestant's father
catching a few Z's

her fourth wedding ...
the guests making sure all gifts
are returnable

unleashed Great Dane
in a New York subway car
draws little notice

proudly displaying
his comic book collection
to nervous in-laws

laundry day surprise ...
body piercing business card
found in the dryer

Side by Side

Gandhi & Garbo, Tolstoy & Tolkien.
Hippocrates & Hitler, Mozart & Motown.
Lincoln & Limbaugh, slavery & slapstick.
Moses & morphine, Plato & plastics.
Raphael & Rasputin, Jesus & Jersey City.

Encyclopedias
Make strange bedfellows.

Waiting

Peripatetic adolescent
in a tight faux-leopard skirt
soliciting on the sidewalk
across from the senior center
Unaware
that the elders observe
and pray for her salvation
every morning and night

A miracle yet to emerge

(*Waiting* was co-written by Styliani Simoneti)

blocked poet
thumbing through dictionaries
hoping for a spark

high school photograph ...
Dad's sideburns drawing guffaws
from his teenaged sons

his wife
reminds him of her birthday
two weeks past

baseball strike ...
old-time socialist cursing
millionaire players

during the vows
the flower girl leering
at the best man

Gramps in his wheelchair,
grandchild on her tricycle
race down the sidewalk

six-year-old pitcher
trying to throw a slider
with a wiffle ball

deep in the attic
grandmother sharpening
her hula hoop skills

obsessive woman
cleaning her house thoroughly
before the maid comes

forty years later
counting the dead relatives ...
wedding photograph

husband and wife
screaming over the meaning
of a comic strip

haiku neurotic
fears his most recent poem
will be his last

aging hippies
giving their baby grandson
a tie-dyed bib

college professor
quoting philosophers
he cannot fathom

before surgery
patient replays in his head
Seinfeld episodes

inner city child
searching for the poetry
in her tenement

crime scene photo ...
beside the chalk outline
a man smiles, waves

freshman advisee
punctuating each sentence
with a nervous laugh

rocket scientist
failing to grasp the genius
of artists, athletes

abused teenager
shocked by the smallest kindness
of her teachers

under *profession*
a pickpocket pencils in
entrepreneur

haiku writer
seeking raw material
on vacation

elderly waitress
showing the new busboys
how to pour water

veteran roofers
sharing remembrances
of their first falls

executive
penciling in a play date
with his infant son

her new neighbor
trimming his toenails
on his front porch

window washers trade
chiropractors' phone numbers
outside the tenth floor

her teenaged son
using his bedroom floor
as closet, hamper

high school teacher
observing the principal
ogling a student

turning over
his parents' framed photograph
before making love

research professor
editing dissertations
on an ocean cruise

home flag at half-staff
commemorating the death
of their pet hamster

nine-year-old girl
orders liver, brussels sprouts …
speechless grandparents

obsessive child
studying the diplomas
on his doctor's wall

elderly sailor
staring at his left bicep …
withered rose tattoo

three generations
at a Marx Brothers film fest
laughing as one

a weary toddler
still trying to befriend
a wary rabbit

mid-session ...
psychiatrist contemplates
dinner options

his five-year-old son
filling crossword puzzle squares
with reds, blues, yellows

baby boomer
shedding tears as she recalls
Captain Kangaroo

wedding crasher
dancing the Macarena
alongside the bride

movie buff's children
refusing to watch a film
shot in black and white

ten-year-old catcher
cleaning off home plate
with his mitt and spit

young psychiatrist
battling his patient's panic
and her HMO

at the pet shop
a four-year-old searches for
the cutest goldfish

Soldiers

Lester sells soap—a dollar
For two bars of Jergens or three bars of Dial—
That he steals from motels.
Giovanni sells reefer;
Mr. Williams, coke and heroin.
Jiggles sells clubs for cars at $10 a piece,
Swearing they're genuine.
Scotty sells cab vouchers, $20 booklets
at half price.
David doesn't sell anymore—too ravaged
by AIDS.

On the first floor of the high-rise, they
Sit around playing cards, smoking, spitting,
Bending forward at the table, looking dead
serious.
As if they're planning some sort of battle,
Whispering to each other the tactical details.

(*Soldiers* was co-written by Styliani Simoneti)

a family dines ...
on their big screen T.V.
carnage from Iraq

summer vacation ...
looking for a low-carb meal
on the boardwalk

Yankee-Met series ...
Bronx and Queens relatives
opening old wounds

high school boy asking
about college scholarships
for skateboarding

Jewish Arkansans
consider naming their son
Bubba Jonathan

master therapist
questioning a new client:
onion-phobic man

sleepless new father
applying shaving cream
to his armpits

New York tourist
searching throughout Idaho
for a decent knish

recent immigrant
staring in amazement ~
male potency ads

saintly Bronx boy
refusing to belittle
Cubs or Red Sox

old professor
grappling with the suicide
of his first student

his nine-year-old son
molding *Crest* toothpaste dabs
into breath mints

for Halloween
painting his bald head green ~
stick deodorant

shock and anger ...
a child calling her *Ma'am*
for the first time

teenager's birthday ...
his grandfather giving him
pairs of suspenders

at the carnival
grandmother, mother, and child
awaiting tattoos

beer-guzzling Mets fan
sits on the cotton candy
dropped by his daughter

biophysicist
uncertain of the spelling
of his newborn's name

Isn't he gorgeous? ...
looking at his new grandson
her Dad replies, *No*

Yankee Stadium ...
asking a hot dog vendor
for some cole slaw

criminal court …
the defendant imagines
the judge naked

little league catcher
tired of squatting, requests
a beanbag chair

fifth grade graduates …
blossoming girls beside
stick-figured boys

private prayers …
Jewish boy puts on his head
a baseball cap

periodontist
explaining his career choice:
I've always loved gums

demented mother
exposing her genitals
to his new wife

their son ponders
whether a wiffle bat
can be corked

daydreaming
of winning a Nobel Prize
he drops his menus

chemistry final ...
a freshman in the back row
snoring softly

indigent mother
filling her baby's bottle
with cherry cola

after four years
asking her analyst
if he is married

masquerade party …
a rabbi dressed head to toe
in black leather

graduate student
contemplating lunch options:
candy bar or chips

a freshman offers
a missed-exam excuse:
I lost my car

illiterate man
dreams of reading to his son
a bedtime story

high school sophomore
searching for a part-time job
that's cool, high-paying

final exam eve ...
reading every other page
in the assigned texts

college freshman
comforting his parents:
a D is passing

sweet sixteen party ...
each girl's belly button
is exposed, pierced

Afghani woman ~
under a thick, black burka
tear-stained cheeks

at the funeral
his grandsons first learning
of his ex-wives

two-year-old actor
sucking his pacifier
between takes

under the boardwalk
licking frozen custard
during a hailstorm

dying grandmother …
with her last, labored breath
insults her children

astrophysicist
visiting the math teacher
who gave him an F

A haiku is composed of two ingredients: an event or experience and the poet's heart expressed through language. It is the combination that makes the haiku itself into an event worth sharing.

Lee Gurga (2003)

In haiku, the words should be so exact that the reader forgets them and only the intuition remains.

Robert Spiess (1999)

summer softball game ...
child throws a brushback pitch
to his mother

underachiever
hoping someday to become
a minor leaguer

their two-year-old son
happily shares his sandwich
with a horde of ants

cloudless summer day ...
grandfather and child indoors
playing pinochle

optimistic boy
trying to teach his dachshund
to catch a frisbee

father of the bride
flashing back to her birth
during their dance

in pink chiffon
topped with a feathered boa ...
nun on New Year's eve

old Persian cat
continuing to torment
a cross-eyed spaniel

beloved elder
instructing his granddaughter
how to cheat at cards

French restaurant ...
their six-year-old requesting
fries and toast

author's mother
reading aloud to him
from his latest book

physics professor
explaining to his students
why a curve ball breaks

taking his date
to the high school prom
in his Dad's taxi

adult siblings
spending a week together
assume their old roles

indulgent father
granting his five-year-old's wish:
her own cell phone

child psychologist
wearing her long, gray hair
in ribboned pigtails

schizophrenic men
discuss the mental illness
of the nursing staff

frantic mother
removing packing peanuts
from her toddler's mouth

neighbor's chihuahua
frightening their children
and German shepherd

his sons debating
which *M&M* tastes best:
red, blue, or yellow

post staff meeting ...
chief psychiatrist unwinds
with the inpatients

teen daughter's bedroom
reeking of the after-shave
of her new boyfriend

during childbirth
becoming more certain
of God's existence

seven-year-old boy
asking to install wind chimes
in his clothes closet

senryu writer
doing a crossword puzzle
as a warm-up drill

in a deep sleep
crying out for his mother ...
fifty-year-old man

English teacher
corrects misspelled graffiti
on the men's room wall

dance school recital ...
six-year-old ballerinas
reinvent vaudeville

pro baseball players
sharing curses and insults
from their native lands

high school senior
on a bus with bad shocks
applies mascara

first-time patient
staring at his doctor's mouth ...
nicotine-stained teeth

reading, savoring
precisely seven haiku
every evening

their china closet ...
baseball bobbleheads beside
porcelain pheasants

matzo ball wars ...
grandmothers and great aunts
compare recipes

businessman
married to his ex-mistress
seeks a replacement

procrastinator ...
fear of failing overwhelms
anger, shame, guilt

arachnologist
rereading *Charlotte's Web*
during his lunch break

four generations
of migrant workers applaud
their first college grad

broad-tailed hummingbird
sipping wildflowers' nectar ~
a winged rainbow

Jewish mother
teaching her Chinese in-laws
how to make kreplach

Wimbledon final ...
ladies in white dresses,
tattooed shoulders

thirty years married
still side-stepping the question
Do I look fat?

Japanese steakhouse ...
their chef juggling raw eggs
with a spatula

in the hospital
with strep ~ his haiku seeds
needing nourishment

his first opera ...
laughing hysterically
at horned Vikings

funeral service
for a practical joker ...
unsure audience

IRS chief
reports having been bullied
as a teenager

old mechanic
humming Cole Porter tunes
during a lube job

Chinese restaurant ...
after the fortune cookies,
requests a divorce

on the boardwalk
a teenager's shorts drooping
dangerously low

after a fight
identical twin brother
shaves off his mustache

August afternoon ...
ladybug sunning itself
on a maple leaf

dining on the beach ...
fried dough, two candy apples
and a six-pack

terrified child ...
one year into therapy
still wearing her coat

summer employer
writing a check, sweat dripping
on his signature

Robin

One day, in the early morning
her neighbors became alarmed
discovering that she had painted
all the apartment doors
pink

They do not misunderstand her
for she goes through cycles
of mania and despair,
sometimes bearing her breasts
sitting by her window for hours
waiting for the security guards
to fall in love with her
as she is with them

On her more lucid days
she rocks gently in an old chair
and nearly asks for help

(*Robin* was co-written by Styliani Simoneti)

child prodigy
explaining the new tax laws
to his accountant

overwhelmed freshmen ...
their only questions concern
what's on the final

naptime,
fearing the dark
he sings to himself

post break-up ...
throwing away six bottles
of moisturizer

spending the evening
staring at his baby's toes ...
first-time father

flight to Utah ...
asking the attendant
if he can land drunk

college weightlifter
holding hands with a girlfriend
one-third his girth

center fielder
being asked to pitch
the nineteenth inning

inept mugger
accepts a personal check
from his victim

full-bearded man
shaving half of his face
for Halloween

after the death
of their only daughter
tearing up his will

poor family
stops in a four-star hotel
for the postcards

their sixteen-year-old
on his first solo drive
hits a police car

biology class …
a student plays tic-tac-toe
on his girlfriend's leg

his father bragging:
My son's going to Harvard …
the one near Boston

during the exam
mathematics professor
playing solitaire

Russian immigrant
learning the new language
from ads, comic strips

her twelve-year-old
writing across the driveway
I need money

over dinner
his daughter, her boyfriend
discuss nipple rings

sorting through
his mother's remains, finding
seven girdles

ornithologist
fantasizes soaring
above the clouds

delivery boy
envisions his face
on the front page

first-year resident
having Christmas dinner
at a pancake house

desperately
trying to reconstruct
a dreamt haiku

two worriers wed ...
both families fearing
for the offspring

before the midterm
three seniors discussing
bikini waxing

run-down diner ...
requesting bottled water
with his scrapple

early morning class ...
a student in the front row
cursing in her sleep

on his lunch break
a young short-order cook
watching Julia Child

kosher deli ...
a Kansas Jew ordering
pastrami on white

again late for school …
helping her drunken father
get washed and dressed

psychotic man
arguing with his pet stick
Woody Jones

first encounter …
his daughter's new boyfriend
sports a gold front tooth

adored grandfather
telling a racist joke
to her fiancé

after breakfast
a youngster planting egg shells
hopes to grow a chick

five-year-old girl
tickling her pet turtle
with a rose petal

on her back porch
composing yet another
sunset haiku

his young grandson
explaining with confidence
the term *lap dance*

embarrassed teen
parking his father's old car
three blocks from school

supermarket aisle ...
finding the condom display
beside the rice cakes

on his deathbed
asking for a copy of
Goethe's *Faust*

Fairbanks, Alaska ...
second-string weatherman
longing for a change

middle-class teacher,
inner-city eighth graders
seeking common ground

Freudian scholar
refusing to acknowledge
he's tunnel-phobic

in his cubicle
under a sea of memos
one autumn haiku

References

Gurga, L. (2003). *Haiku: A poet's guide.* Lincoln, IL: Modern Haiku Press.

Haiku Society of America (1994). *Draft definitions submitted for member comment, January, 1994.* New York: Haiku Society of America.

Priebe, D. (2004). Introduction. *Haiku Headlines,* 17(3), 1.

Spiess, R. (1999). Speculations. *Modern Haiku,* 30(2), 85–86.

Index of Poems' Original Sources

Several of the poems presented in *The Essence of Moments* have been published elsewhere. Listed below are the titles of these poems and the journals and periodicals in which they first appeared.

In **Haiku Headlines:** *eightieth birthday; elderly sailor; elderly smokers; little leaguer; two Nobel winners*

In **Hummingbird: Magazine of the Short Poem:** *Waiting*

In **Muse of Fire:** *Hope*

In **The Pegasus Review:** *conservationist; fourth of July; her six-year-old son; Maryland hopscotch; on the rear bumpers; recycle day*

In **Up Dare?:** *Robin; Soldiers*

In **Welcome Home:** *fifth grade graduates; naptime*

Author's Note

Born and raised in New York City, Robert H. Deluty received his B.A. from New York University and his M.A. and Ph.D. (in Clinical-Community Psychology) from the State University of New York at Buffalo. Since 1980, he has been a psychology professor at the University of Maryland, Baltimore County; in 2002, he was named UMBC's Presidential Teaching Professor. He resides in Ellicott City, Maryland with his wife, Barbara (a clinical psychologist) and their children, Laura and David.